Harriet Tubman's ESCAPE

A FLY on the WALL HISTORY

BY THOMAS KINGSLEY TROUPE   ILLUSTRATED BY JOMIKE TEJIDO

PICTURE WINDOW BOOKS
a capstone imprint

Hi, I'm Horace, and this is my sister, Maggie.

We've been "flies on the wall" during important events in history.

We watched countless people build the Great Wall of China.

We saw Karl Benz build the first car.

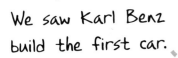

We even saw men carve the faces on Mount Rushmore!

One adventure we'll never forget was when we made a daring escape with Harriet Tubman in the mid-1800s ...

In the summer of 1848, we found ourselves near a farm in Bucktown, Maryland. It was a time when slavery was legal throughout the southern United States. People could own other people. Slaves were forced to work without pay and often under terrible conditions.

We saw a group of slaves working in the field. An angry-looking man took a worker aside. He beat him and told him to work harder.

I don't like this, Horace.

Why don't the slaves just leave?

They can't. Their ancestors were taken from their homes in Africa thousands of miles away.

They're like prisoners. They have no money or way to escape.

Those who DO try to escape face

* * *

Slavery in the United States began in 1619. People from Africa were first brought to what is now the state of Virginia. There they were enslaved.

The farm was the Brodess plantation. It was run by a man named Edward Brodess. Most of the slaves looked skinny, like they didn't get enough to eat.

Maggie and I watched Mr. Brodess take two slaves away from the group. They were unhappy where they were, but they were even more unhappy to be taken away. They were going to be sold to another plantation.

That boy and girl are teenagers. And they are treated like property!

What about their families?

Keeping families together isn't super important to slave owners.

They just want the farm work to get done.

★ ★ ★

Because slaves were considered property, most slave owners didn't keep track of birthdays or family members. Families were often broken apart to work on other plantations.

★ ★ ★

One slave woman had a big scar on her head. Her name was Harriet Tubman. She looked really sleepy. I buzzed in her ear to try to keep her awake.

"Don't fall asleep, Minty," another slave told her. "The overseer will get angry again."

"It's hard," Harriet said. "My head is playing with me. It doesn't know it's not time to rest."

Whoa, what happened to her head? —

When Harriet was younger, an angry overseer threw a heavy weight at a runaway slave.

But instead of hitting the runaway, the weight hit Harriet. It hurt her head really badly.

⋆ ⋆ ⋆

Harriet Tubman was born sometime around 1822. Her real name was Araminta Harriet Ross. Her nickname growing up was "Minty."

Maggie and I heard the news the following spring. Mr. Brodess had died. Harriet worried about what his death might mean for her and the other slaves. His widow, Eliza Brodess, now owned them. She could do whatever she pleased.

You'd think that when an owner dies, his slaves would be free.

Sadly, no. Enslaved people are considered property, just like cattle, land, or furniture. Surviving family members get them.

When Eliza dies, her kids will own the slaves ... and all the children born of the female slaves.

Harriet knew Mr. Brodess owed money. She was sure she and her brother and sister would be sold to other owners. Her family would be broken apart. Harriet knew she had to do something. But she didn't know what. Maggie and I didn't know what to do either.

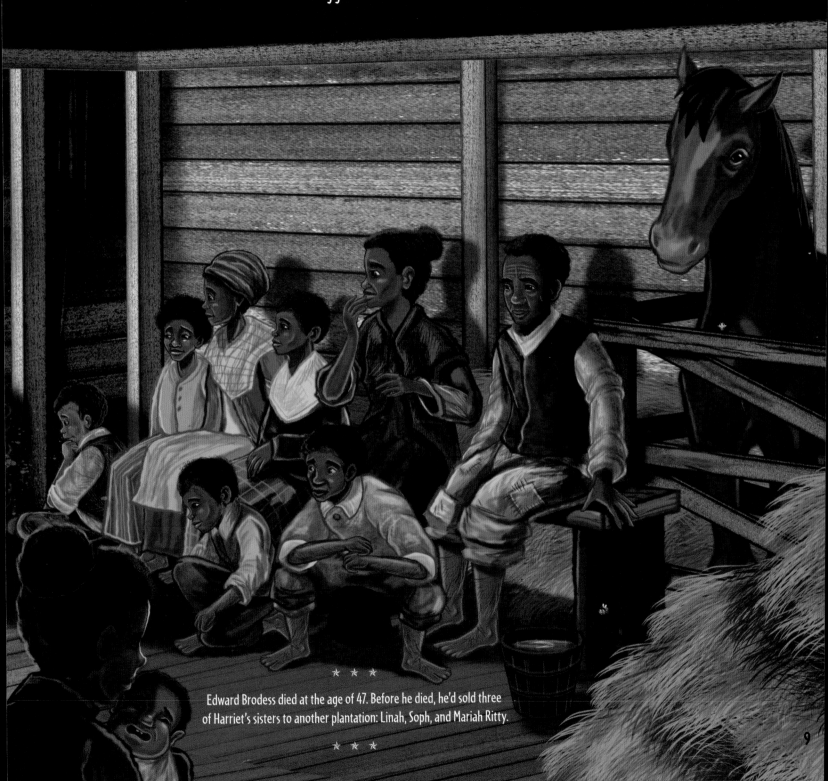

* * *

Edward Brodess died at the age of 47. Before he died, he'd sold three of Harriet's sisters to another plantation: Linah, Soph, and Mariah Ritty.

* * *

A few months later, Harriet started to plan her escape. She had to get away from the plantation. She wanted to be free. And she wanted her family to join her.

I hope Harriet can catch a ride on the Underground Railroad.

The funny thing is, I haven't seen any train tracks nearby ...

Well, it's not a real train, Maggie.

The Underground Railroad is a secret group of people. They help runaway slaves.

They give them food, clothing, and safe places to rest on their journey.

She had heard others talking about the Underground Railroad. She learned that the railroad helped enslaved people find freedom. It moved them north, to the "free" states. Some people even went as far north as Canada.

⋆ ⋆ ⋆

Maryland slaves feared being sold to slave owners in the Deep South. The living and working conditions there were often much worse.

⋆ ⋆ ⋆

Harriet talked about her plan with her husband, John. He had been a slave once, but now he was a free man. Harriet told John she was afraid of being sold.

"Come with me," Harriet said. "Help me find freedom."

⋆ ⋆ ⋆

Not much is known about Harriet's husband, John.
It's even unknown if they had children together.

⋆ ⋆ ⋆

But John said no. He didn't like Harriet's plan. He said he'd report his wife to her master if she tried to leave.

So Harriet backed down. She got quiet and promised she wouldn't go.

What? Just like that, Harriet's going to give up?

I don't think so, Maggie.

I think Harriet is going to be sneaky about her escape!

Late one September night, Maggie and I heard whispering. Harriet was waking Ben and Henry, her two younger brothers. Together the three of them snuck out of the barn and ran across the field. (Maggie and I flew alongside.) They crawled under a fence and disappeared into the woods.

I'm nervous for Harriet and her brothers. I hope they can escape without any trouble!

Me too, Horace.

But it's really dark! How are they supposed to find the Underground Railroad?

Harriet and her brothers didn't get far. Ben and Henry thought they were going the wrong way. They were afraid of what would happen if they got caught. Harriet begged them to keep going. But they said no. All of them headed back.

A week or so later, Harriet snuck out again. This time she went on her own.

I wish Henry and Ben would go with Harriet.

You wouldn't leave me like that, would you?

No way.

And don't worry. Harriet might be little, but she's got a strong will.

Something tells me she knows what she's doing!

* * *

Harriet was only 5 feet (1.5 meters) tall. Despite her size, she was tough and strong from years working in the fields.

* * *

Maggie and I joined Harriet. We stayed off the main roads and hid whenever someone came by.

At night we used the North Star as a guide. Harriet knew the North Star always pointed north. She planned to follow it until she reached the free state of Pennsylvania. During the day she slept and looked for other clues that pointed north.

Pennsylvania?
That's a really long walk.

Or wings!

You're right!
If only she had a horse!

Or a REAL train to ride!

I don't know how far we'd gone, but Maggie and I were getting tired. Harriet was too. A woman saw Harriet walking nearby and called her over. She invited her inside.

The woman was part of the Underground Railroad. She gave Harriet some food and a safe place to rest. When it was time to go, the woman pointed her toward the next "station."

I thought Harriet was in trouble when that woman called her over.

Me too!
I'm glad Harriet wasn't too scared to talk to the lady.

The Underground Railroad will help her head north more safely.

★ ★ ★

Houses where runaway slaves could hide on the Underground Railroad were called stations or depots. A conductor was a person who helped move people from station to station.

★ ★ ★

Harriet ran through forests and waded through swamps. People from the Underground Railroad hid her in their barns and wagons. It made me happy to see people treat Harriet like a person.

Even with the help, the journey was hard on Harriet. She had to run at night and sleep during the day. She missed her family. She wondered how others back on the plantation were doing.

How much farther is it to Pennsylvania?

Are we still in Maryland?

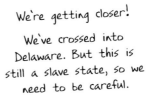

We're getting closer!

We've crossed into Delaware. But this is still a slave state, so we need to be careful.

★ ★ ★

Wilmington, Delaware, was the last stop on the Underground Railroad for slaves escaping north.

★ ★ ★

Finally, Harriet, Maggie, and I crossed the Pennsylvania state line. We had made it to a free state. Harriet stopped and looked at her hands in wonder. She thought she was dreaming.

Later, when thinking back on that moment, she would say, "There was such a glory over everything. I felt like I was in heaven."

✳ ✳ ✳

No one knows exactly how long Harriet's journey took.
It might have taken anywhere from 10 days to 3 weeks on foot.

✳ ✳ ✳

We continued on to Philadelphia. There Harriet met members of the Pennsylvania Society for the Abolition of Slavery. They helped her find a home and a fresh start. She got a job cleaning houses and saved some money. Maggie and I helped when we could.

Although Harriet was free from slavery, she wasn't happy. She thought about the family she'd left behind. She thought about other slaves stuck farther south. She started working on a new plan—a plan to give others the gift of freedom.

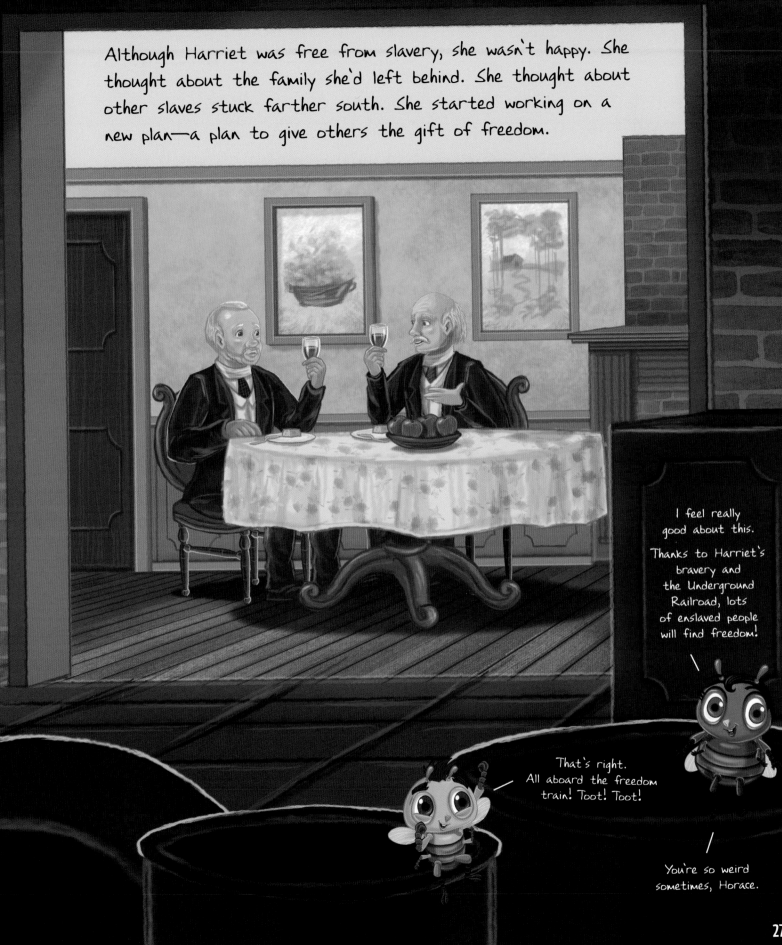

I feel really good about this.

Thanks to Harriet's bravery and the Underground Railroad, lots of enslaved people will find freedom!

That's right. All aboard the freedom train! Toot! Toot!

You're so weird sometimes, Horace.

Harriet Tubman didn't sit still for long. In December 1850, she received a message that her niece Kessiah and her children were going to be sold. Harriet set out for Maryland. She rescued her niece's family and led them to freedom.

Harriet became a conductor for the Underground Railroad. She returned to the South many more times and helped more than 100 enslaved people find freedom. She learned many tricks to slip past slave catchers.

Harriet Tubman never lost a passenger. She never let anyone give up on his or her dream of freedom.

TIMELINE

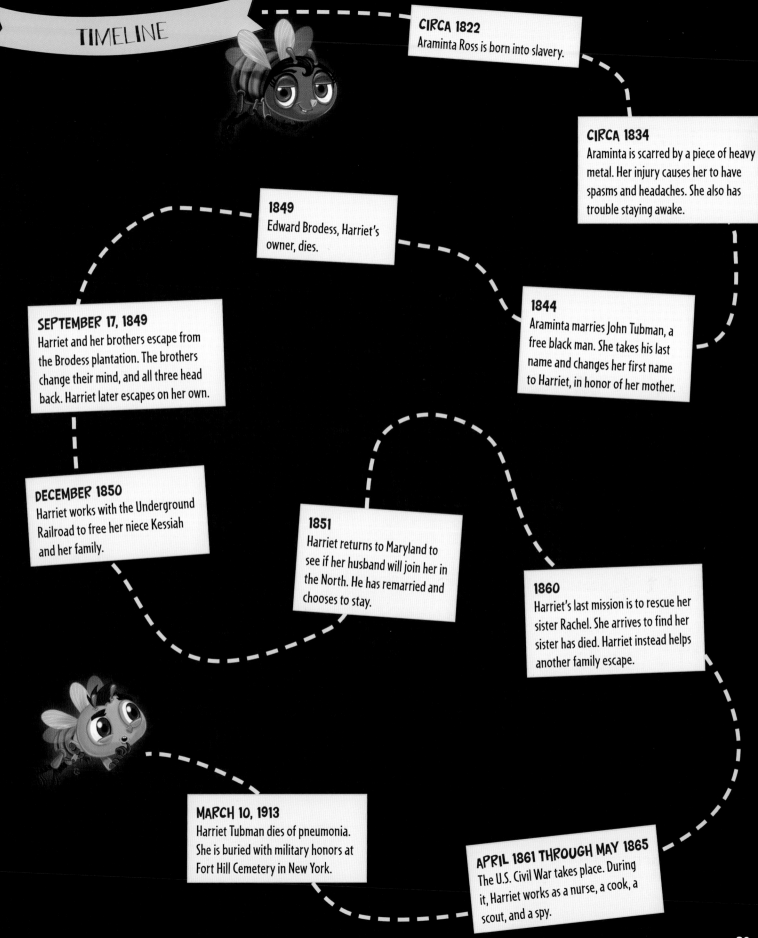

CIRCA 1822
Araminta Ross is born into slavery.

CIRCA 1834
Araminta is scarred by a piece of heavy metal. Her injury causes her to have spasms and headaches. She also has trouble staying awake.

1849
Edward Brodess, Harriet's owner, dies.

1844
Araminta marries John Tubman, a free black man. She takes his last name and changes her first name to Harriet, in honor of her mother.

SEPTEMBER 17, 1849
Harriet and her brothers escape from the Brodess plantation. The brothers change their mind, and all three head back. Harriet later escapes on her own.

DECEMBER 1850
Harriet works with the Underground Railroad to free her niece Kessiah and her family.

1851
Harriet returns to Maryland to see if her husband will join her in the North. He has remarried and chooses to stay.

1860
Harriet's last mission is to rescue her sister Rachel. She arrives to find her sister has died. Harriet instead helps another family escape.

MARCH 10, 1913
Harriet Tubman dies of pneumonia. She is buried with military honors at Fort Hill Cemetery in New York.

APRIL 1861 THROUGH MAY 1865
The U.S. Civil War takes place. During it, Harriet works as a nurse, a cook, a scout, and a spy.

29

GLOSSARY

abolition–the end of something, such as slavery

ancestor–a member of a person's family who lived a long time ago

conductor–a person who leads or guides; people who helped runaway slaves escape to the North on the Underground Railroad were called conductors

Deep South–usually the region that includes the states of Alabama, Georgia, Louisiana, Mississippi, and South Carolina

enslave–to make someone a slave

enslaved people–men, women, and children owned by other people

legal–allowed by the rules

overseer–a person who keeps watch over and directs the work of others, especially slaves or laborers

plantation–a large farm where crops such as cotton and sugarcane are grown

scar–a mark left on the skin by a cut or burn that has healed

slavery–the owning of other people; slaves are forced to work without pay

THINK ABOUT IT

1. Describe some of the hardships enslaved people in the southern United States faced in the mid-1800s. (Key Ideas and Details)

2. What specific event pushed Harriet to plan her escape to freedom in 1849? Why would that event have made Harriet so worried? (Key Ideas and Details)

3. Harriet's brothers were too scared to continue when they first tried to escape. Why do you think Harriet went back to the plantation with them? (Integration of Knowledge and Ideas)

READ MORE

Barton, Jen. *What's Your Story, Harriet Tubman?* Cub Reporter Meets Famous Americans. Minneapolis: Lerner Publications, 2016.

Kolpin, Molly. *Great Women of the Civil War.* The Story of the Civil War. North Mankato, Minn.: Capstone Press, a Capstone Imprint, 2015.

Meister, Cari. *Follow the Drinking Gourd: An Underground Railroad Story.* Night Sky Stories. North Mankato, Minn.: Picture Window Books, 2013.

INTERNET SITES

FactHound offers a safe, fun way to find Internet sites related to this book.
All of the sites on FactHound have been researched by our staff.

Here's all you do:
Visit *www.facthound.com*
Type in this code: 9781479597888

Check out projects, games and lots more at
www.capstonekids.com

INDEX

Look for all the books in the series:

Special thanks to our adviser, Kevin Byrne, PhD, Professor Emeritus of History, Gustavus Adolphus College, for his expertise.

Picture Window Books is published by Capstone,
1710 Roe Crest Drive, North Mankato, Minnesota 56003
www.mycapstone.com

Library of Congress Cataloging-in-Publication Data
Names: Troupe, Thomas Kingsley, author | Tejido, Jomike, illustrator.
Title: Harriet Tubman's escape : a fly on the wall history / by
  Thomas Kingsley Troupe.
Description: North Mankato, Minnesota : Picture Window Books, an imprint
  of Capstone Press, 2017. | Series: Nonfiction picture books. Fly on the wall
history | Includes bibliographical references and index. | Audience:
  K–Grade 3. | Audience: 6–8.
Identifiers: LCCN 2016034402 | ISBN 9781479597888 (library binding) |
  ISBN 9781479597925 (paperback) | ISBN 9781479597963 (ebook (pdf))
Subjects: LCSH: Tubman, Harriet, 1820?–1913–Juvenile literature. | Slaves–
  United States–Biography–Juvenile literature. | African Americans–
  Biography–Juvenile literature. | Underground Railroad–Juvenile literature.
Classification: LCC E444.T82 T75 2017 | DDC 306.3/62092 [B]–dc23
LC record available at https://lccn.loc.gov/2016034402

Editor: Jill Kalz
Designer: Sarah Bennett
Creative Director: Nathan Gassman
Production Specialist: Steve Walker

The illustrations in this book were planned with pencil on paper and finished with digital paints.

Printed and bound in the USA
010059S17CG